THE FUTURE'S SO BRIGHT, I CAN'T BEAR TO LOOK

NATION
BOOKS

A Member of the Perseus Books Group

Copyright © 2008 by Tom Tomorrow
Published by Nation Books, A Member of the Perseus Books Group
116 East 16th Street, 8th Floor
New York, NY 10003

Nation Books is a co-publishing venture of the Nation Institute and the Perseus Books Group

Books published by Nation Books are available at special discounts for bulk purchases in the
United States by corporations, institutions, and other organizations. For more information, please contact
the Special Markets Department at the Perseus Books Group, 2300 Chestnut Street, Suite 200,
Philadelphia, PA 19103, or call (800) 810-4145, ex. 5000,
or e-mail special.markets@perseusbooks.com.

A CIP catalog record for this book is available from the Library of Congress.
ISBN 978-1-56858-402-7
LCCN 2008928497
10 9 8 7 6 5 4 3 2 1

"The Republican Guide to Successful Supreme Court Nominations" (pp. 6-7)
and "Bill O'Reilly's Very Useful Advice for Young People" (pp. 127-129)
originally appeared in the *Village Voice*. A "dramatic" reading of the latter
by Keith Olbermann can probably still be found by searching
YouTube, and is worth the effort.

Cover design by Tom Tomorrow
www.thismodernworld.com

for Beverly: world enough and time

and for Nicholas: you're gonna fly

ALSO BY TOM TOMORROW

INTRODUCTION

From my vantage point, in the penthouse suite high atop Tomorrowco's world-famous skyscraper headquarters in beautiful downtown Dubai, the future looks pretty bright indeed. My personal assistant tells me that a lot of you people are having some sort of problems with your mortgages and your gas prices and so on, but I really can't be bothered with any of that—I'm much too busy managing my business holdings and partying with fabulous celebrity friends like P. Diddy and Paris Hilton (who made the most amusing remark last night as we were sipping champagne in a hot tub filled with more champagne, but I guess you had to be there, and of course you weren't).

To be honest, I have no idea what the title of this book means. I've long since relinquished the actual production of Tomorrowco's flagship product, "The Modern World," to the extremely talented artists and writers of the Huazi Reform Through Labor Camp in Liaoning Province. I'll bet you didn't know that! Or maybe you did—it's possible that one of the actors I send out to do personal appearances and interviews in my name has mentioned it at some point. You never know what those guys are going to say!

But the Tomorrowco Board of Directors thought it would be appropriate for me to write this introduction, so as to give this book the "personal touch" you readers apparently crave, when you are not worrying about your mortgages and the price of gasoline and whatever else it is you worry about. Speaking of which—you know what I like to do when I'm feeling stressed out? Splash around with some of my supermodel friends in the Olympic-sized pool on the rooftop of the Tomorrowco building! It's very relaxing! You should try it sometime, if you ever get the opportunity, which of course you will not.

Now, Tomorrowco has obviously branched out significantly from our humble origins in political cartooning, diversifying into many different areas—running shoes, microprocessors, bootleg DVDs, health insurance, internet pornography, our popular chain of "Sparky's Penguinburger" restaraunts ("A Literally Inestimable Number Sold!"), and of course our 34 percent ownership stake in the Pentagon.

And make no mistake, we're always looking ahead to the future. Though we unloaded our mortgage-backed securities last year (and just in time—boy did we make a killing!), we remain extremely active in the speculative energy, food, and water markets, and are looking into ways to turn the Earth's very atmosphere into a tradable commodity. The future's so bright, I have to wear the expensive sunglasses my close personal friend Bono gave me after our legendary impromptu late-night jam session with Vladimir Putin! But that's another story entirely.

Still—despite all the changes the years have brought, we here at Tomorrowco haven't forgotten where we came from, and in the interests of "keeping it real," we are extremely pleased to make this latest compilation of "The Modern World" cartoons available to you. My personal assistant's personal assistant assures me that the cartoon strips contained herein are amusing indeed, and I have no reason to doubt her. I'm looking forward to reading them, as you undoubtedly are as well!

I could go on all day, but my personal jet is fueled and waiting to take me across town for an important meeting with the next president of the United States. (The election's five months away, but I already know who's going to win! That's just how things work, when you're as rich as I am, which of course you are not.)

So in closing, let me offer some heartfelt advice to young cartoonists just starting out in this fabulous profession for which we share such a common passion: don't worry about a thing—success is guaranteed! There is literally no more lucrative field you can enter—and if you focus on that rarified strata known as alt-weekly political cartooning, well, the sky's the limit! So good luck to you, and enjoy your journey to the inevitable fortune and fame that await you!

Tom Tomorrow
July 2008

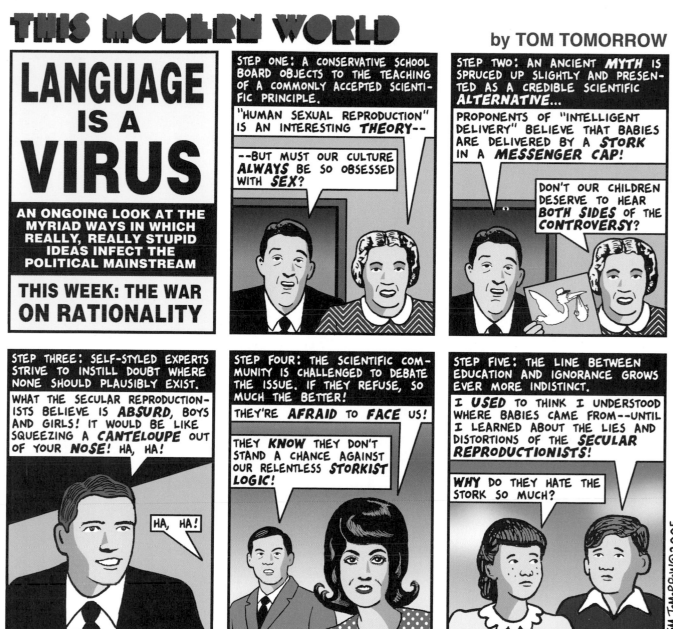

3

4

THE REPUBLICAN GUIDE TO SUCCESSFUL SUPREME COURT NOMINATIONS

FEATURING KARL ROVE

NOTE: BECAUSE NO NOMINEES HAVE BEEN ANNOUNCED AS OF THIS WRITING, WE HAVE ELECTED TO USE A VARIETY OF HISTORICAL AND/OR FICTIONAL PERSONAGES AS PLACEHOLDERS. THE READER SHOULD ATTRIBUTE NO DEEPER "MEANING" TO THEIR SELECTION, WHICH WAS BOTH RANDOM AND ARBITRARY.

HELLO, REPUBLICANS--I'M *KARL ROVE!* AS YOU KNOW, WE'RE ABOUT TO SELECT *TWO NEW SUPREME COURT JUSTICES!*

IT'S AN *HISTORIC* OPPORTUNITY, AND WE MUST BE SURE TO SELECT REPLACEMENTS WHO ARE SUFFICIENTLY *EVIL*--ER, I MEAN TO SAY, SUFFICIENTLY COMMITTED TO *CORE CONSERVATIVE VALUES!*

THE DEMOCRATS WILL WHINE NO MATTER *WHO WE SELECT*--SO *WHY FUCK AROUND?*

NO DOUBT ABOUT IT, JUDY--THE NOMINATION OF ADOLF HITLER'S ZOMBIE CLONE* IS *SURE* TO INFLAME LIBERAL SENSIBILITIES!

THANKS FOR THE INSIGHT, ANNOYING CNN ANALYST GUY!

*REMEMBER--JUST AN ARBITRARY STAND-IN, WITH NO PARTICULAR SIGNIFICANCE.

AFTER ALL--THE MORE THEY BITCH AND MOAN, THE EASIER IT WILL BE TO PORTRAY THEM AS *DIVISIVE EXTREMISTS!*

ER--DO YOU *REALLY* THINK THE ZOMBIFIED CLONE OF A NAZI LEADER IS AN APPROPRIATE CHOICE FOR THE *SUPREME COURT?*

"*NAZI*"! YOU SAID "*NAZI*"! I SUPPOSE YOU THINK *ALL* CONSERVATIVES ARE NAZIS, DON'T YOU? *DON'T YOU?!*

ER--I--

BY THE TIME *WE'RE* THROUGH, WE'LL HAVE THE DEMOCRATS BEGGING FOR *FORGIVENESS!*

SNIF! WE'RE--WE'RE *SORRY* WE ACCUSED ADOLF HITLER'S ZOMBIE CLONE--AND BY EXTENSION, OUR BRAVE TROOPS IN IRAQ--OF BEING *NAZIS!*

NOT THAT SMOOTH SAILING IS *GUARANTEED*, OF COURSE! THE DEMOCRATS MAY STILL CHOOSE TO UTILIZE THE *FILIBUSTER!*

HE'S THE UNDEAD CLONE OF HISTORY'S WORST MASS MURDERER! OF *COURSE* WE'RE GOING TO BLOCK THE NOMINATION!

SORRY--YOU AGREED TO ONLY DO THAT UNDER *EXTRAORDINARY* CIRCUMSTANCES! I DON'T SEE ANYTHING EXTRAORDINARY HERE--DO *YOU* FELLAS?

EVERYTHING LOOKS NORMAL TO *ME!*

JUST ANOTHER DAY IN THE SENATE!

CONT'D

7

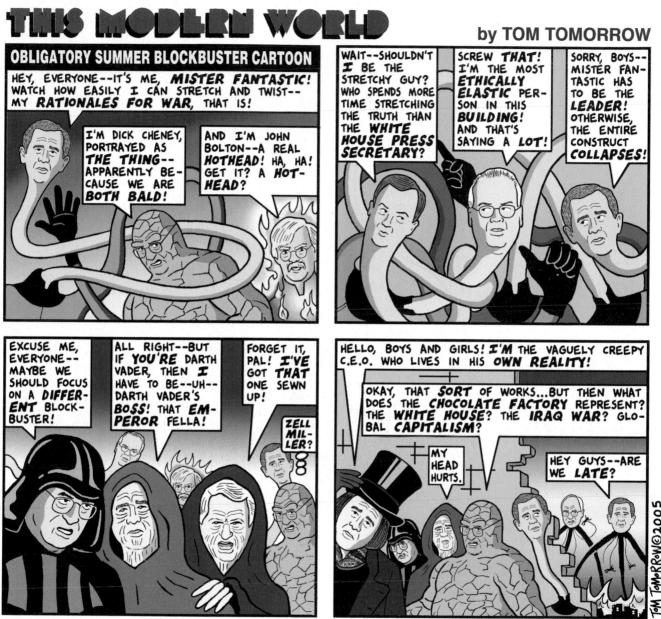

THIS MODERN WORLD

by TOM TOMORROW

Occam's Razor: the principle which states that the simplest explanation is generally best.

IN ORDER TO BELIEVE THAT THE BUSH ADMINISTRATION DOES NOT SANCTION THE USE OF *TORTURE*--

WHICH IT *CERTAINLY* DOES NOT!

YOU'D HAVE TO BE A TERROR-LOVING LIBERAL ELITIST TO SUGGEST *OTHERWISE!*

--YOU MUST *ALSO* BELIEVE THAT RESPONSIBILITY FOR ABU GHRAIB REALLY *DOES* REST WITH A MERE HANDFUL OF *BAD APPLES*--

ALL OF WHOM HAVE BEEN APPROPRIATELY PUNISHED, END OF STORY.

I SEE NO NEED TO EVER SPEAK OF THE MATTER AGAIN.

--AND THAT REPORTS FROM FBI AGENTS OF ABUSE AT GUANTANAMO ARE SIMPLY NOT *CREDIBLE*--

I BET THE *M.S.M.* QUOTED THEM COMPLETELY OUT OF *CONTEXT!*

WHAT IF BY "SHACKLED TO THE FLOOR IN A POOL OF FILTH" THEY ACTUALLY MEANT "RELAXING IN A BIG COMFY *BED*"?

--AND THAT THE BRUTAL DEATHS OF PRISONERS AT BAGRAM AND QAIM CAN ONLY BE BLAMED ON A *FURTHER* HANDFUL OF BAD APPLES--

I THINK THE FACT THAT WE EVEN *KNOW* ABOUT THESE DEATHS--

--IS PROOF THE SYSTEM *WORKS!*

AND ANYTHING WE *DON'T* KNOW ABOUT-- DIDN'T *HAPPEN!*

--*AND* THAT LOW-RANKING BAD APPLES AT EACH FACILITY JUST *HAPPENED* TO DEVELOP THE SAME SPECIFIC TECHNIQUES OF ABUSE AND HUMILIATION, INDEPENDENT OF ONE ANOTHER.

IT'S JUST ONE OF THOSE *CRAZY COINCIDENCES!*

OR IT WOULD BE, IF IT WERE TRUE. WHICH OF COURSE IT IS NOT.

FORGET OCCAM'S RAZOR--THIS IS MORE LIKE OCCAM'S *SLEDGE-HAMMER.*

IT'S LIKE *I* ALWAYS SAY--THE MOST *CONVOLUTED AND UNLIKELY* EXPLANATION IS USUALLY BEST.

AS LONG AS IT FAVORS *US*.

WHICH IT ALMOST ALWAYS DOES.

ODDLY ENOUGH.

NEXT: EXTRAORDINARY RENDITION-- OR *FREE SURPRISE VACATION?*

TOM TOMORROW ©2005

14

16

18

THIS MODERN WORLD

by TOM TOMORROW

Panel 1:

G.O.P. POWERBROKER *JACK ABRAMOFF* HAS BEEN INDICTED FOR DEFRAUDING CLIENTS OUT OF MILLIONS. ABRAMOFF HAS ALSO BEEN INDICTED, ALONG WITH FORMER BUSINESS PARTNER *ADAM KIDAN*, ON FRAUD CHARGES RELATED TO THEIR PURCHASE OF THE *SUNCRUZ GAMBLING FLEET*.

NOW, NOW--WE SHOULDN'T JUMP TO *CONCLUSIONS*--

Panel 2:

ABRAMOFF AND KIDAN FEUDED WITH SUNCRUZ'S SELLER--UNTIL HE WAS *GUNNED DOWN* IN 2001. TWO OF THE THREE MEN RECENTLY ARRESTED FOR THAT MURDER RECEIVED A PAYMENT OF NEARLY $250,000 FROM KIDAN--WHO SAYS IT WAS FOR "*LEGITIMATE BUSINESS EXPENSES*."

I SEE NO REASON TO *DOUBT* HIM--

Panel 3:

ABRAMOFF ALSO PICKED UP THE TAB FOR A TRANSATLANTIC GOLF TRIP FOR HIS CLOSE PERSONAL FRIEND *TOM DELAY*--WHO, OF COURSE, IS HIMSELF FACING MULTIPLE INDICTMENTS FOR CONSPIRACY AND MONEY LAUNDERING IN TEXAS.

ON A RELATED NOTE, ADMINISTRATION OFFICIAL *DAVID SAFAVIAN* WAS JUST ARRESTED FOR OBSTRUCTING AN INVESTIGATION INTO THAT TRIP.

IT'S OBVIOUSLY A *PARTISAN WITCH HUNT*--

Panel 4:

MEANWHILE, *BILL FRIST* IS BEING INVESTIGATED FOR INSIDER TRADING...AND WE SHOULD FIND OUT ANY DAY NOW IF THE SPECIAL PROSECUTOR INVESTIGATING THE LEAK OF *VALERIE PLAME'S* IDENTITY INTENDS TO BRING ANY INDICTMENTS IN *THAT* CASE...

NO BIGGIE--I MEAN-- THERE'S NOTHING--ER-- THAT IS--UH--*SPLUTTER*--

Panel 5:

KA-BOOM!

URK!

Panel 6:

I SUPPOSE YOU ENJOYED THAT.

IN DIFFICULT TIMES LIKE THESE, IT'S *IMPORTANT* TO SAVOR THE SMALL PLEASURES LIFE HAPPENS TO SEND YOUR WAY.

I'M FINE... DON'T WORRY... NO PROBLEMO...

TOM TOMORROW©2005

20

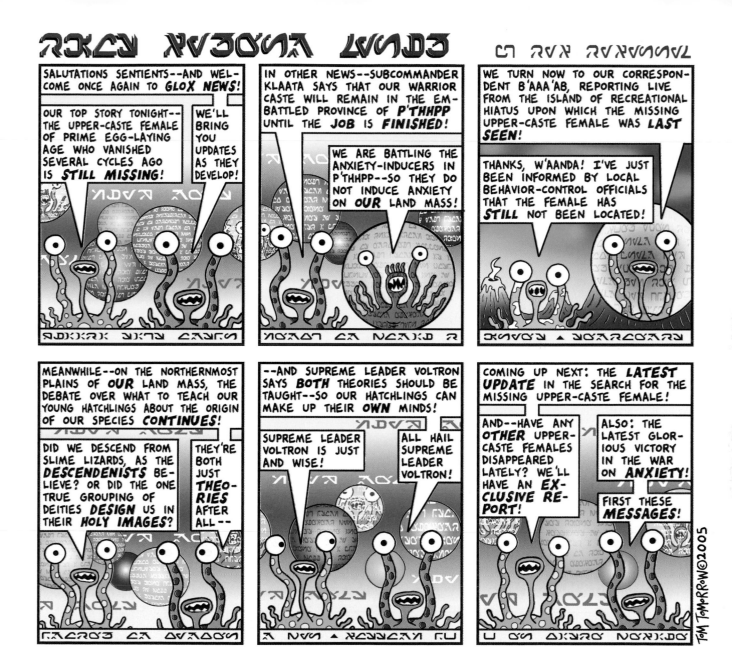

21

22

25

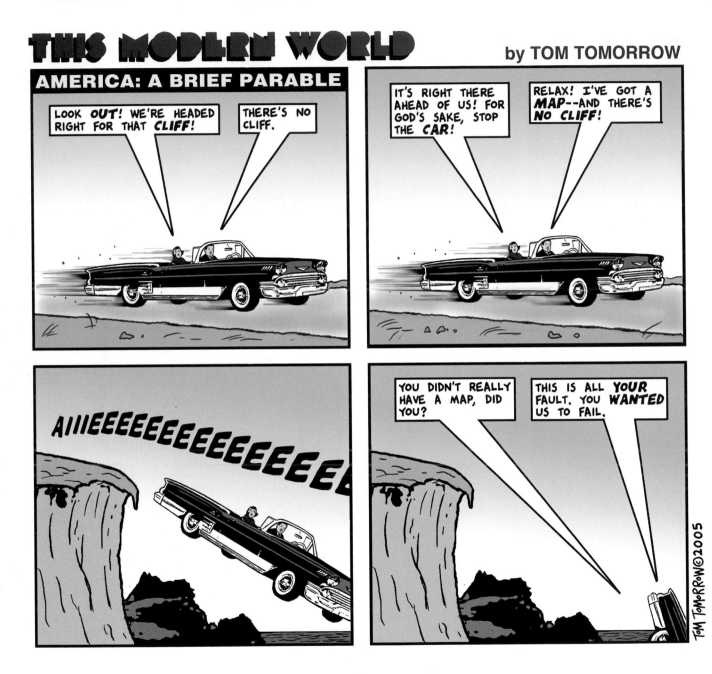

29

THIS MODERN WORLD

by TOM TOMORROW

This week: it's time for another installment of...

It's Just That Simple:

Easy Answers for Your Troublesome Questions!

Q: Why was there an 18-hour delay before the press was informed that the Vice President had shot a man in the face?

A: Because Dick Cheney wanted the story to be as "accurate as possible!"

IF THERE'S ONE THING THE VICE PRESIDENT IS KNOWN FOR, IT IS HIS COMMITMENT TO *ACCURACY!*

THE LAST THING HE WOULD *EVER* WANT TO DO IS *MISLEAD* ANYONE!

It's just that simple!

Q: How did news of warrantless NSA spying hurt national security? Didn't al Qaeda already know their phones might be tapped?

A: Yes--but if the media weren't constantly reminding them about it, they might forget!

WE ARE SO ABSENT-MINDED--SOMETIMES WE FORGET TO *EAT* FOR DAYS AT A TIME!

IT'S A GOOD THING *BREATHING* IS AN AUTONOMIC FUNCTION, OR ELSE WE'D BE IN *SERIOUS* TROUBLE!

It's just that simple!

Q: The administration was warned about the breached levee the night Hurricane Katrina hit New Orleans. So why was the government so sluggish in its response to the disaster?

A: It was all Brownie's fault!

WHEN PRESIDENT BUSH SAID "HECKUVA JOB, BROWNIE," HE WAS *OBVIOUSLY* BEING *SARCASTIC!*

LIBERALS HAVE *NO* SENSE OF IRONY!

It's just that simple!

Q: Do they really think we're stupid enough to believe these lame excuses--or do they just not care what we think?

A: Both!

HEH, HEH! IT'S *JUST THAT SIMPLE!*

NOW STOP ASKING SO MANY QUESTIONS--BEFORE SOMEBODY ELSE GETS MISTAKEN FOR A PEN-RAISED *GAME BIRD.*

IF YOU KNOW WHAT I MEAN.

TOM TOMORROW©2006

32

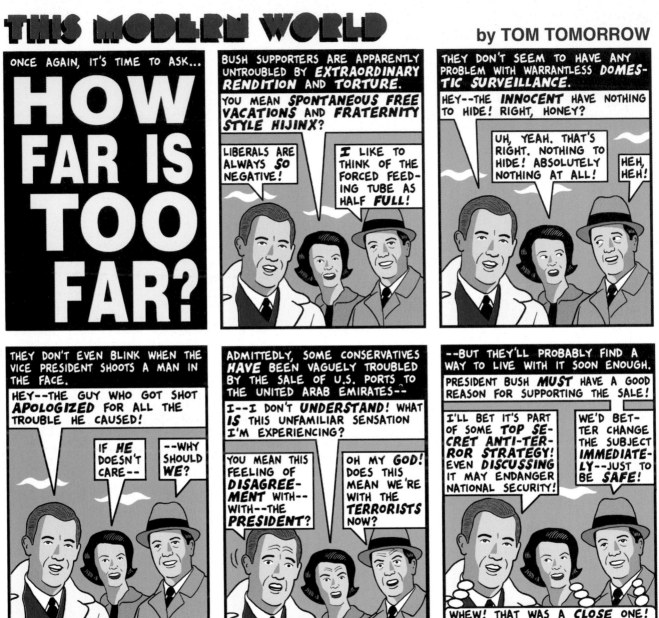

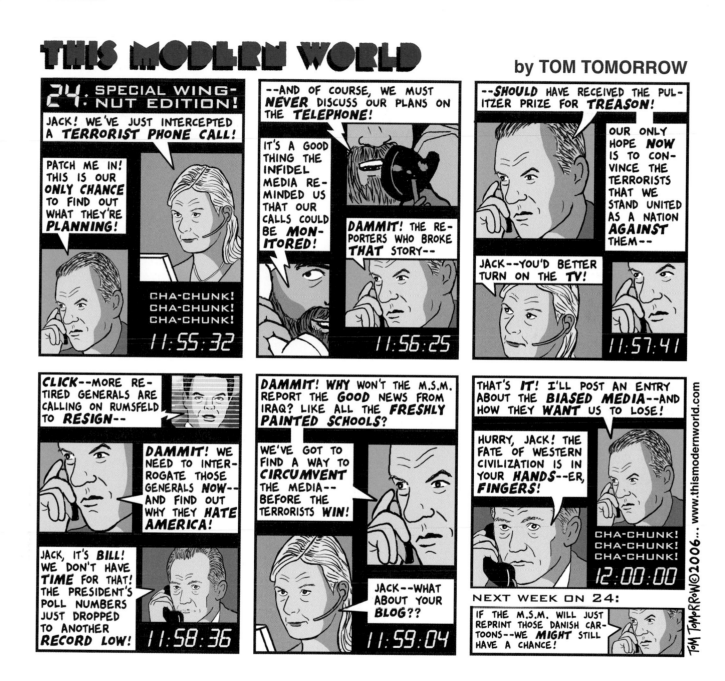

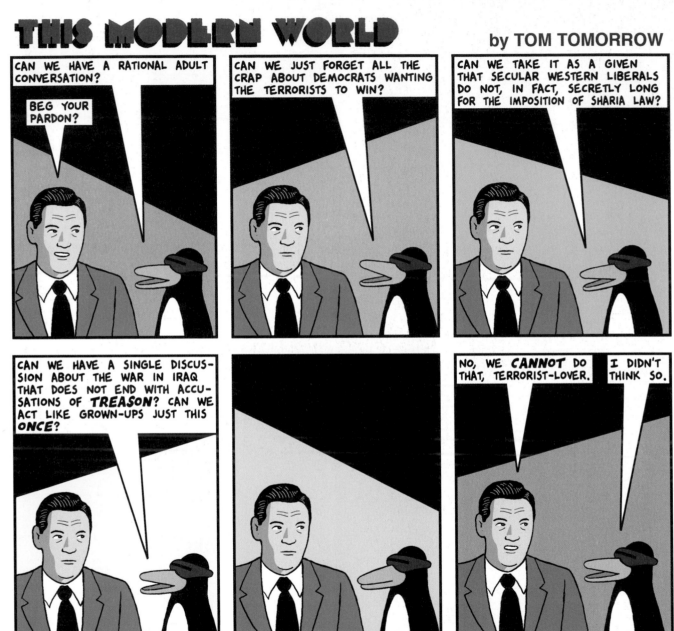

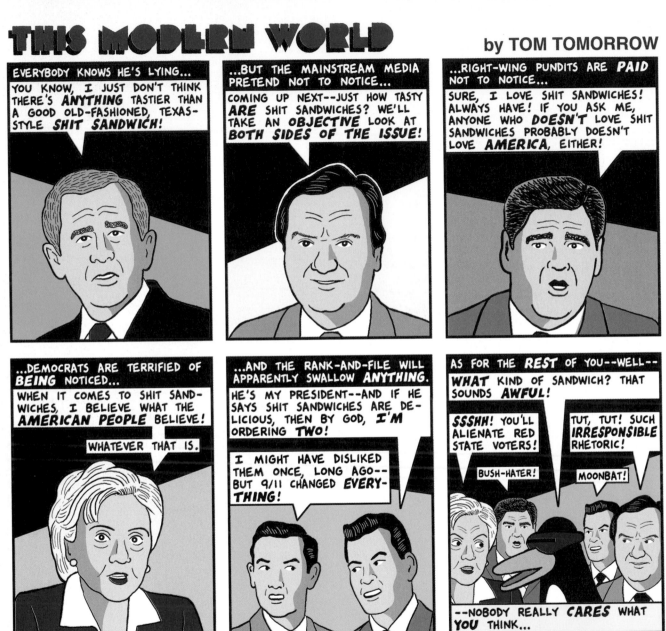

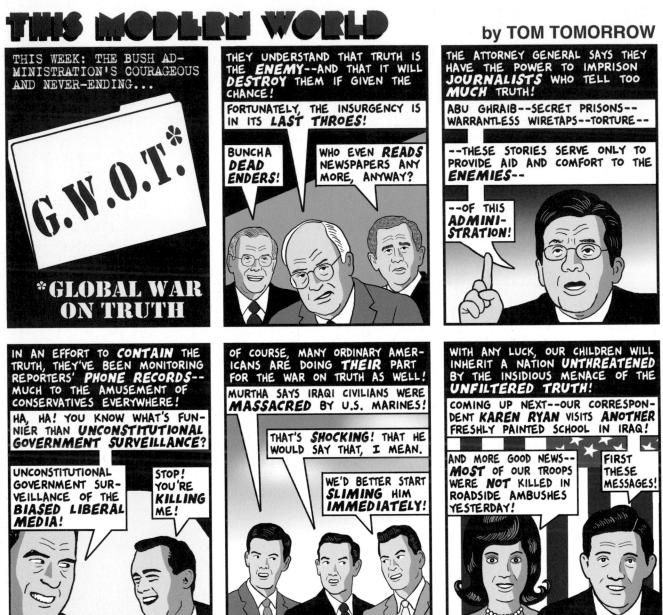

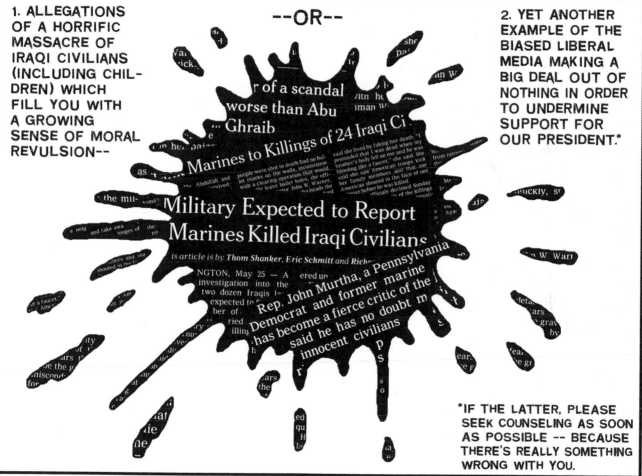

50

52

54

THIS MODERN WORLD

by TOM TOMORROW

WELCOME TO THE RIGHTWINGOVERSE

SO THE FAR LEFT NUTJOBS DISAGREE WITH KINDLY OLD JOE LIEBERMAN ON *ONE SMALL ISSUE*--AND THEY *PURGE* HIM FROM THEIR PARTY IN A *LIBERAL WITCH-HUNT!*

THESE HATE-ADDLED LUNATICS HAVE USHERED IN A NEW ERA OF *PARTISAN POLARIZATION!* I GUESS WE CAN *FORGET* ABOUT THE SPIRIT OF *CIVILITY* AND *BIPARTISANSHIP* REPUBLICANS HAVE WORKED SO HARD TO *FOSTER* THESE PAST SIX YEARS!

SAY WHAT?

AND THE *NAMES* THEY CALLED HIM! THE TERRIBLE, TERRIBLE *NAMES!* THEY CALLED HIM NAMES SO DREADFUL, I CAN'T EVEN *REPEAT* THEM! IN FACT, I HAVEN'T EVEN *READ* THEM! I DON'T KNOW WHAT THEY WERE--AND I DON'T *WANT* TO KNOW! DAVID BROOKS SAYS THEY WERE SIMPLY *AWFUL*--AND THAT'S GOOD ENOUGH FOR *ME!*

AFFABLE JOE LIEBERMAN WAS THE VICTIM OF AN ONLINE *JIHAD!* IT WAS A *LIBERAL INQUISITION* CONDUCTED BY *FAR LEFT BLOG-OFASCISTS* WHO WILL ACCEPT NOTHING LESS THAN *COMPLETE IDEOLOGICAL PURITY!*

THIS IS A DISASTER OF *UNPRECEDENTED* PROPORTIONS! THE VERY LEGITIMACY OF OUR *DEMOCRACY* HAS BEEN THROWN INTO QUESTION!

IN OTHER WORDS, A MAJORITY OF CONNECTICUT DEMOCRATS VOTED FOR THE CANDIDATE THEY PREFERRED.

WHOA! PLEASE--TRY TO CONTAIN YOUR *UNDILUTED LIBERAL RAGE!*

IT'S LIKE STARING INTO AN *OPEN BLAST FURNACE!*

A VERY *ANGRY* BLAST FURNACE!

SIGH...

TOM TOMORROW©2006

61

73

THIS MODERN WORLD

by TOM TOMORROW

interlude

NEW YEAR'S ALREADY. I CAN'T BELIEVE HOW QUICKLY THE SEASONS FLY BY.

I MEAN, YOU BARELY MANAGE TO GET THE AIR CONDITIONERS PUT AWAY BEFORE THE YARD IS KNEE DEEP IN LEAVES.

AND AS SOON AS YOU GET THE LEAVES RAKED UP, IT'S SUDDENLY TIME TO START SHOVELLING THE SNOW.

YOU DO THAT FOR A COUPLE OF MONTHS, AND THEN BAM! IT'S SPRING, AND YOU'RE SCRAMBLING TO GET YOUR TAXES DONE ON TIME.

AND THEN IT'S SUMMER AGAIN AND YOU PULL THE AIR CONDITIONERS OUT OF THE BASEMENT AND START ALL OVER AGAIN.

THE YEARS ARE GOING BY SO FAST I BARELY HAVE TIME TO CATCH MY BREATH ANYMORE.

I FEEL LIKE I'M ON A CARNIVAL RIDE SPINNING OUT OF CONTROL. MY KID'S GONNA BE GROWN UP AND GONE BEFORE I KNOW IT.

YOUR CHILD IS THREE YEARS OLD.

MY POINT *EXACTLY!*

TOM TOMORROW©2006

77

81

90

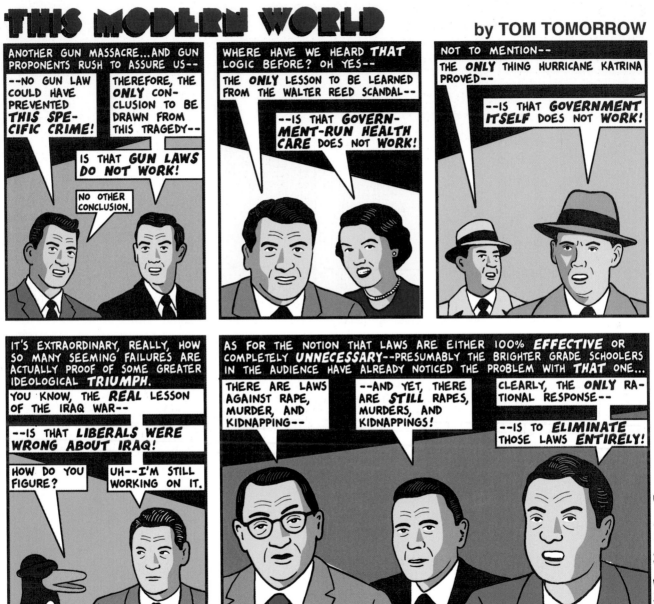

94

100

101

103

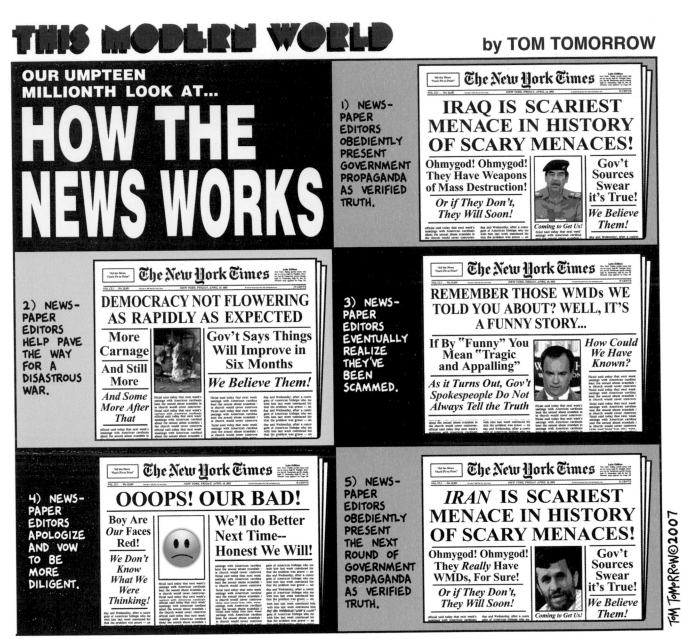

105

110

111

THIS MODERN WORLD

by TOM TOMORROW

A FEW THINGS WE'VE BEEN WONDERING ABOUT LATELY

1) SHOULD WE ASSUME THAT *EVERY* SANCTIMONIOUS, MORALIZING REPUBLICAN IS A CLOSETED SEXUAL LIBERTINE--OR JUST *MOST* OF THEM?

HOLY COW, LOOK AT THE *TIME!* I'VE GOT TO GIVE A SPEECH ON THE IMPORTANCE OF TRADITIONAL FAMILY VALUES IN AN *HOUR!*

2) HOW UTTERLY WRONG ABOUT EVERYTHING CAN A CONSERVATIVE PUNDIT *BE*--AND STILL BE TREATED WITH DEFERENCE AND RESPECT?

--IRAQ WILL BE AN OVERWHELMING *SUCCESS*--IRAN AND SYRIA WILL BOW TO OUR *WILL*--

--AND *EVERYONE* WILL GET A *FREE PONY!*

WOW! I'VE ALWAYS *WANTED* A *FREE PONY!*

3) ALONG WITH EVOLUTION AND GLOBAL WARMING, WHAT *OTHER* COMMONLY-HELD SCIENTIFIC PRINCIPLES DO THE MAJORITY OF G.O.P. PRESIDENTIAL CANDIDATES CONSIDER QUESTIONABLE?

AERODYNAMICS, SHMAERODYNAMICS! THIS PLANE IS HELD ALOFT BY *GOD'S HEAVENLY ANGELS!*

YES SIR. LET'S NOT MENTION THAT TO THE PRESS, SIR.

4) DOES ANYONE *REALLY* BELIEVE THAT GENERAL PETRAEUS' SEPTEMBER ASSESSMENT OF THE SURGE WILL CONTAIN ANY SURPRISES?

I *WONDER* WHAT HE WILL SAY!

THERE'S NO WAY TO *KNOW*--AND THERE'S NO POINT IN EVEN *MENTIONING* IRAQ UNTIL *THEN!*

5) WHAT EXACTLY *DOES* DICK CHENEY KEEP IN HIS "MAN-SIZED SAFE"?

PRAY YOU NEVER FIND OUT! *BWAH HA HA HA HA!*

I THINK--*GULP*--IT'S ALMOST *FEEDING TIME*, MISTER CHENEY!

TOM TOMORROW©2007

THIS MODERN WORLD
by TOM TOMORROW
THIS WEEK: A "HANDY" GUIDE TO THE HOUSING MARKET--FEATURING THE INVISIBLE HAND OF THE FREE MARKET!
IF YOU'RE INVISIBLE, HOW COME I CAN SEE YOU?
IT'S THE MAGIC OF THE MARKET, SON! NOW--LET'S GET STARTED!
BACK IN THE OLDEN DAYS, BANKERS USED TO INSIST ON ALL SORTS OF "DOCUMENTATION" BEFORE THEY'D GIVE SOMEONE A HOUSING LOAN--EVEN IF THAT PERSON REALLY WANTED A LOAN!
BUT THEN I INTERVENED--INTRODUCING THOSE BANKERS TO MY FRIENDS ON WALL STREET, WHO STARTED BUYING MORTGAGE LOANS FROM BANKS AND SELLING THEM TO INVESTORS!
THINGS BEGAN TO LOOSEN UP WHEN LENDERS NO LONGER HAD TO WORRY ABOUT PETTY DETAILS LIKE BEING REPAID! AND EVENTUALLY THE SUBPRIME MARKET TOOK OFF--AND THEN WHAT A PARTY WE HAD!
RATES WERE LOW, MONEY WAS PLENTIFUL, AND HOUSING PRICES SKYROCKETED--ER--I MEAN TO SAY, ROSE TO THEIR PROPER VALUATION, AS DETERMINED BY THE INHERENT RATIONALITY OF THE FREE MARKET!
HEH, HEH.
YEAH, THINGS WERE GOING GREAT--UNTIL MILLIONS OF BORROWERS INEXPLICABLY BEGAN TO DEFAULT ON THEIR LOANS! NO ONE COULD HAVE SEEN THAT COMING!
BUT WASN'T IT INEVITABLE THAT--
AHEM! ABSOLUTELY NO ONE! BUT NOT TO WORRY! AS ALWAYS, THE INVISIBLE HAND OF THE FREE MARKET HAS THE SOLUTION!
WHICH IS...?
A MASSIVE GOVERNMENT BAILOUT! PROBLEM SOLVED! ON TO THE NEXT OPPORTUNITY!
I GOTTA SAY, YOU DON'T SEEM VERY RATIONAL TO ME.
TELL IT TO THE HAND, KID.
TOM TOMORROW©2007... www.thismodernworld.com

115

THIS MODERN WORLD
by TOM TOMORROW
THE QUEST FOR COMMON GROUND
FEATURING
THE SENSIBLE LIBERAL
and
THE RIGHTWING NUTCASE
THE REAL PROBLEM WITH POLITICS TODAY IS ALL THE PARTISAN BICKERING! IT'S TIME FOR CONSERVATIVES AND LIBERALS TO WORK TOGETHER--TO GET THINGS DONE!
I COULDN'T AGREE MORE!
REALLY?
SURE! LET'S GET STARTED RIGHT NOW! I BELIEVE WE SHOULD STAY IN IRAQ INDEFINITELY! HOW ABOUT YOU?
WELL--I BELIEVE WE SHOULD START TO THINK ABOUT SOME SORT OF WITHDRAWAL--
THEN THE COMPROMISE IS OBVIOUS--WE'LL STAY IN IRAQ INDEFINITELY!
BUT-- UH-- WHAT?
IT'S SETTLED THEN! MOVING RIGHT ALONG--
--I BELIEVE WE SHOULD IGNORE THE THREAT OF GLOBAL WARMING! WHAT SAY YOU?
ER--I BELIEVE WE SHOULD NOT--
OKAY THEN! LET'S PUT POLITICS BEHIND US--
--AND IGNORE GLOBAL WARMING! BOY, THIS IS GREAT! CAN'T YOU JUST FEEL THE UNITY?
BUT--THESE ARE NOT COMPROMISES--
OH, I SEE--
--YOU'RE TOO WEDDED TO YOUR OBSOLETE PARTISAN AGENDA TO THINK OUTSIDE THE BOX! SORRY I WASTED YOUR TIME WITH MY TWENTY-FIRST CENTURY POST-PARTISAN APPROACH!
NO--WAIT! I'LL TRY HARDER!
WEELLLL--
--OKAY! LET'S WORK TOGETHER--AND FIGURE OUT THE BEST WAY TO BAN GAY MARRIAGE, BLOCK HEALTH CARE REFORM, CHIP AWAY AT ABORTION RIGHTS, AND BUILD A WALL ALONG THE MEXICAN BORDER!
WITHOUT ANY PARTISAN BICKERING?
I WOULDN'T HAVE IT ANY OTHER WAY.
TOM TOMORROW©2007

119

123

BILL O'REILLY'S VERY USEFUL ADVICE FOR YOUNG PEOPLE

AS CHANNELED BY VILE LEFT-WING SMEAR MERCHANT **TOM TOMORROW**

HELLO, I'M *BILL O'REILLY!* YOU KIDS MAY THINK OF ME AS A CREEPY OLD GUY FROM THE *TEEVEE*--

--BUT IF YOU BUY MY NEW BOOK, "KIDS ARE AMERICANS TOO," YOU'LL LEARN THAT I'M ACTUALLY A "HIP" AND "WITH IT" GUY WHO CAN REALLY "RELATE" TO THE "YOUNG GENERATION"-- AND I'M HERE TODAY TO *PROVE* IT! SO LET'S GET *STARTED!*

TOPIC #1: DATING!

AS YOU YOUNG PEOPLE MATURE, YOU'LL START NOTICING THE OPPOSITE SEX! YOU'LL FIND YOUR-SELVES WANTING TO SPEND MORE *TIME* TOGETHER!

YOU *BOYS* MAY EVEN BE TORMENTED BY THE URGE TO CALL YOUNG LADIES ON THE PHONE TO DISCUSS HYPOTHETICAL SEXUAL ACTIVITIES IN A MANNER THAT *SOME* PEOPLE MIGHT CONSIDER INAPPROPRIATE.

I ADVISE AGAINST THIS.

TOPIC #2: FRIENDSHIP!

EVERYONE LIKES TO HAVE FRIENDS--BUT SOME-TIMES FRIENDS DISAGREE! IF *YOU* HAVE AN ARGUMENT WITH YOUR FRIENDS, HERE'S WHAT YOU SHOULD DO: CALL THEM *COWARDS* UNTIL THEY AGREE TO APPEAR ON YOUR SHOW--AND THEN, IF YOU DON'T LIKE WHAT THEY SAY, *CUT THEIR MICROPHONES!*

WHAT ARE THEY GONNA *DO*, WHINE ABOUT IT ON SOME *BLOG*?

WHICH BRINGS US TO OUR *NEXT* TOPIC--

TOPIC #3: THE INTERNET!

I KNOW THAT YOU YOUNG PEOPLE ENJOY USING THE *COMPUTERS*--BUT ALWAYS RE-MEMBER THAT THE INTERNET IS A *VERY DANGEROUS PLACE!* IT'S FILLED WITH *VILE HATEMONGERS* WHO SPREAD LIES AND DISTORTIONS ABOUT *ME*--BILL O'REILLY!

www.thesmokinggun.com

The Smoking Gun

Mackris v. O'Reilly

IF YOU EVER RUN ACROSS THESE LIES, WHICH ARE SOMETIMES PRESENTED IN THE FORM OF LEGAL FILINGS, SHUT DOWN YOUR COMPUTER IMMEDIATELY, TAKE IT OUTSIDE, AND THROW IT IN THE PATH OF THE FIRST ONCOMING VEHICLE YOU SEE.

KA-CHUNK!

IF YOUR PARENTS ASK WHAT HAPPENED, BLAME IT ON A COMPUTER VIRUS.

CONT'D ☞

TOPIC #4: MY RATINGS!

ONE THING THAT'S VERY IMPORTANT FOR YOU YOUNG PEOPLE TO UNDERSTAND AS YOU SET OUT ON YOUR JOURNEY THROUGH LIFE IS THAT *MY RATINGS ARE MUCH HIGHER THAN KEITH OLBERMANN'S!*

MY RATINGS

OLBERMANN'S RATINGS

AND THAT'S NOT THE *ONLY* THING ABOUT ME THAT'S BIGGER! BUT THAT'S A TOPIC FOR A FEW YEARS FROM NOW, WHEN YOU'RE OLD ENOUGH TO ENJOY A HARMLESS, NON-CREEPY DOUBLE ENTENDRE!

TOPIC #5: BRITNEY SPEARS'S PANTIES!

SHE KEEPS *LOSING* THEM! WHAT'S UP WITH *THAT*? HA, HA!*

?!

* I MAKE A SIMILARLY HILARIOUS JOKE WITHIN THE FIRST FEW PAGES OF "KIDS ARE AMERICANS TOO"! ANYONE WHO TELLS YOU THIS IS CREEPY SHOULD BE IGNORED, BECAUSE THEY ARE LYING.

TOPIC #6: FALAFELS!

THEY'RE A DELICIOUS MIDDLE EASTERN FOOD STAPLE, NOT TO BE CONFUSED WITH FIBROUS BATH SPONGES! A LITTLE ADVICE FOR YOU *FELLAS*--DEFINITELY DON'T TAKE ANY FALAFELS INTO THE SHOWER, OR SUGGEST TO ANY YOUNG LADIES THAT YOU WOULD LIKE TO DO SO! *THAT'S* A MISTAKE YOU'LL REGRET FOR THE REST OF YOUR *LIFE!*

TRUST ME ON THIS ONE.

TOPIC #7: FAMILY!

WHAT'S MORE IMPORTANT TO YOU THAN YOUR *FAMILY*? EXCEPT MAYBE ME, BILL O'REILLY? AND THAT'S WHY WE MUST NEVER, EVER ALLOW THE DEMOCRATS TO LEGALIZE *GAY MARRIAGE!* BECAUSE THE NEXT THING YOU KNOW, PEOPLE WOULD BE MARRYING *GOATS!* WOULD YOU LIKE TO HAVE A GOAT FOR A PARENT?

OF COURSE YOU WOULD NOT.

TOPIC #8: SAN FRANCISCO!

YOUNG PEOPLE FREQUENTLY ASK ME, "MISTER O'REILLY, SIR--WHY DO SAN FRANCISCANS HATE AMERICA SO MUCH?" AND I SAY, "THEY JUST *DO*--AND WE SHOULD JUST LET THE TERRORISTS BLOW THEM *ALL UP!*" AND THAT'S ALL YOU NEED TO KNOW ABOUT *THAT* VILE CITY!

POP QUIZ!

Let's see if you've been paying attention!

1. Who has a bigger penis, Bill O'Reilly or Keith Olbermann?

2. What is the difference between a loofah and a falafel? Discuss and memorize.

3. Explain why you can't trust anything you read on the Internet about me, Bill O'Reilly.

TOPIC #9: SEX!

SEX IS A VERY SPECIAL THING THAT HAPPENS BETWEEN A MAN AND A WOMAN WHO ARE MARRIED, AND IS ALSO SOMETHING THAT AN EMPLOYER MAY OCCASIONALLY DISCUSS ON THE PHONE WITH SUBORDINATES OF THE OPPOSITE GENDER, IN A PERFECTLY INNOCUOUS AND NON-CREEPY WAY!

WHERE'S THE HARM IN IT, I ASK YOU! WHAT KIND OF CRAZY PSYCHO LOON WOULD BE OFFENDED BY *THAT*?

NONETHELESS, YOU YOUNG PEOPLE SHOULD UNDERSTAND THAT SOMETIMES PEOPLE RECORD PHONE CONVERSATIONS WITHOUT *TELLING* OTHER PEOPLE, WHO THEN HAVE TO HAND OVER A LOT OF "BENJAMINS" TO MAKE THE WHOLE MESS GO AWAY.

KEEP IT IN MIND. YOU'LL THANK ME SOMEDAY.

MOVING RIGHT *ALONG*--

?   ?

TOPIC #10: GEORGE SOROS!

YOUNG PEOPLE EVERYWHERE MUST BEWARE THIS SECRETIVE JEWISH FINANCIER WHO CLANDESTINELY CONTROLS THE DEMOCRAT PARTY! HE'S A FAR-LEFT *RADICAL* WHO FUNDS VILE INTERNET WEBSITES FULL OF LIES ABOUT ME, BILL O'REILLY!

YOU KIDS ALREADY KNOW WHAT TO DO IF YOU EVER RUN *ACROSS* ONE OF THOSE WEBSITES, RIGHT?

CONT'D 👉

128

TOPIC #11: THE DAILY KOS!

THIS WEBSITE IS WORSE THAN THE **NAZIS**! IT'S WORSE THAN **MUSSOLINI** AND THE **KKK**! I DECLARE, I'VE NEVER SEEN SO MUCH VILE HATRED IN ONE **PLACE**!

SOMEBODY FETCH THE **SMELLING SALTS**! I FEEL FAINT JUST **THINKING** ABOUT IT!

MERCY **ME**!

NOW, YOU YOUNG PEOPLE CAN DECIDE FOR YOURSELVES WHAT YOU THINK OF DEMOCRAT CANDIDATES WHO BOYCOTT A FAIR AND BALANCED **FOX NEWS DEBATE**--BUT **ATTEND** A VILE, HATE-FILLED **DAILY KOS CONVENTION**! SO GO AHEAD! **DECIDE**!

UH--I THINK THEY ARE NOT FIT TO BE **PRESIDENT**...?

WELL--WHAT AN ASTUTE YOUNG PERSON **YOU** ARE...

..."DAWG"!

TOPIC #12: THE ACLU!

THIS IS THE MOST DANGEROUS ORGANIZATION IN AMERICA TODAY! THEY'RE WORSE THAN AL QAEDA AND THE DAILY KOS **COMBINED**! "ACLU" STANDS FOR **ATHEISTS, COMMUNISTS, AND LIBERALS UNITED**...TO DESTROY EVERYTHING GOOD AND DECENT ABOUT THIS COUNTRY!

YOU CAN LOOK IT UP, THOUGH I WOULD PREFER THAT YOU DID NOT.

MULTIPLE-CHOICE QUIZ!

1. George Soros is...

(a) a vile America-hater; (b) a hate-filled America-hater; (c) a far-left America-hater filled with vile, hate-filled America-hatred; (d) all of the above.

2. Daily Kos bloggers are...

(a) vile America-haters; (b) hate-filled America-hating far-left America-haters; (c) degenerate Soros-funded smear merchants to whom cowardly Democrats are inexplicably in thrall; (d) all of the above.

TOPIC #13: SECULAR PROGRESSIVES!

"SECULAR PROGRESSIVES" ARE PEOPLE LIKE **GEORGE SOROS** AND **LEFT-WING BLOGGERS** WHO WANT TO DESTROY THE WHITE MALE CHRISTIAN POWER STRUCTURE IN THIS COUNTRY! YOU CHILDREN DO NOT WANT TO DESTROY THE WHITE MALE CHRISTIAN POWER STRUCTURE, DO YOU?

OF COURSE YOU DO NOT.

TOPIC #14: TRADITIONALISTS!

"TRADITIONALISTS" ARE PEOPLE LIKE **ME** WHO HAVE THE COURAGE TO STAND **UP** TO "SECULAR PROGRESSIVES"! AND SINCE YOU YOUNG PEOPLE ENJOY USING "SLANG," YOU MIGHT WANT TO NOTE HOW I'VE INVENTED AN ENTIRELY NEW TERMINOLOGY RATHER THAN ACKNOWLEDGE MY OWN FUNDAMENTAL CONSERVATISM! AND I EXPECT THE ENTIRE WORLD TO **EMBRACE** IT--JUST LIKE THEY EMBRACED MY BOYCOTT OF **FRANCE**!

WE BROUGHT THOSE CHEESE-EATERS TO THEIR **KNEES**! YOU CAN READ ABOUT IT IN THE **PARIS BUSINESS REVIEW**!

IF YOU CAN FIND A COPY.

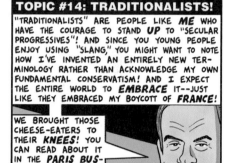

TOPIC #15: CHRISTMAS!

I'M SURE YOU HAVE MANY HAPPY MEMORIES OF CHRISTMASTIME, SINCE YOU ARE YOUNG PEOPLE WHO ENJOY THAT SORT OF THING! WELL, IF **GEORGE SOROS** AND THE **ACLU** HAVE THEIR WAY, THERE WON'T **BE** ANY MORE CHRISTMASTIME!

YOU SEE, THE SECULARISTS HAVE DECLARED A SECRET **WAR** ON CHRISTMAS--AND IT'S **SO** SECRET, I'M PRACTICALLY THE ONLY PERSON WHO **KNOWS** ABOUT IT! BUT IF THEY HAVE **THEIR** WAY, YOU'LL BE STANDING AROUND A "HOLIDAY" TREE NEXT CHRISTMAS, SINGING SONGS ABOUT PAGAN GODS AND EXCHANGING GIFT DONATIONS TO **UNICEF**!

AND I WON'T LET THAT HAPPEN! DO YOU HEAR ME? I **WON'T**!! BECAUSE **I'M** THE ONLY PERSON LOOKING OUT FOR YOU!!!

ME!! **BILL**!! **O**!! **REILLY**!!!

TOPIC #16: CARTOONS ABOUT ME, BILL O'REILLY!

IGNORE THEM! THEY'RE NOT FUNNY! IF YOU WANT A GOOD LAUGH, READ SOME CARTOONS THAT MAKE FUN OF **GEORGE SOROS** AND THE **ACLU**!

OR THAT ONE WITH THE CONSERVATIVE **DUCK**! NOW **THAT'S** WHAT I CALL HUMOR!

OH, AND ONE MORE THING: KEITH OLBERMANN'S PENIS IS REALLY, REALLY TINY.

JUST SAYIN'.

FIN!

TOM TOMORROW©2007

132

THIS MODERN WORLD

by TOM TOMORROW

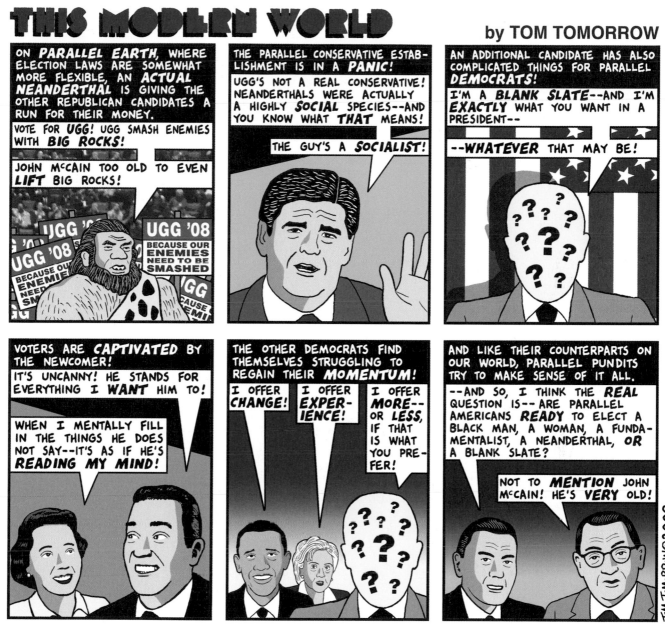

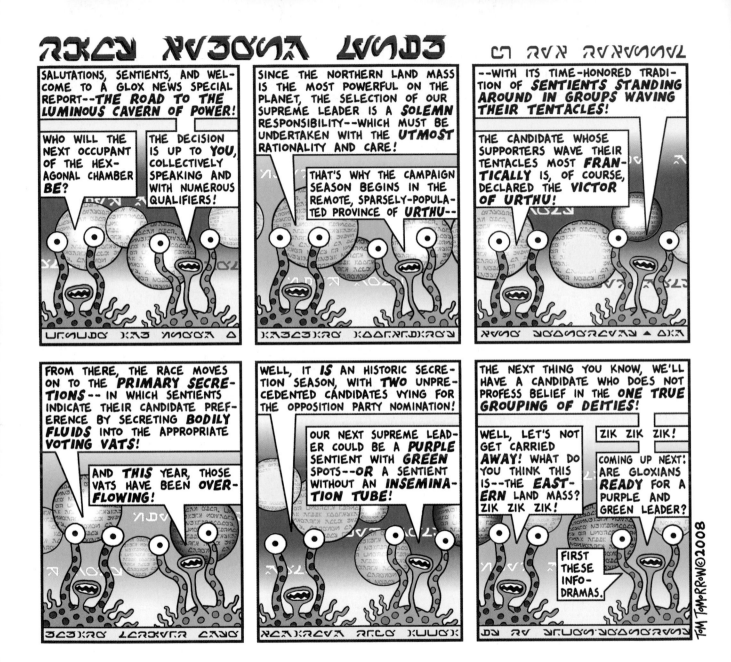

140

141

142

143

THIS MODERN WORLD
by TOM TOMORROW

THE ELITIST MENACE

THEY'VE INFILTRATED THE HIGHEST LEVELS OF OUR SOCIETY--

--AND NOW ONE OF THEM MAY BECOME **PRESIDENT!**

IF THERE'S ONE THING AMERICANS CAN'T **STAND**, IT'S AN **ELITIST**--AND HILLARY CLINTON HAS BEEN WORKING HARD TO PROVE **SHE'S** NOT ONE!

HERE I AM, HAVING A SHOT AND A BEER IN A WORKING CLASS TAVERN--JUST LIKE I **ALWAYS** DO WHEN I NEED TO RELAX!

HEY, ANY-BODY GOT A **GUN?** I JUST **LOVE** GUNS!

AND **PICKUP TRUCKS!** AND, UH, WHATEVER ELSE IT IS YOU PEOPLE LIKE.

BARACK OBAMA, HOWEVER, DOESN'T ALWAYS SEEM TO UNDERSTAND THE **IMPORTANCE** OF THE ISSUE!

YOU WANNA TRY SOME OF OUR DOWN-HOME **DEEP FRIED FAT BALLS**--COVERED IN DELICIOUS **GREASY FAT SAUCE?**

ER--I-- UH--NO THANKS.

WHAT'S THE MATTER? NOT **FANCY** ENOUGH FOR YA--SENATOR **FANCYPANTS?**

AND HIGHLY-PAID MEDIA PROFES-SIONALS REMAIN **AGHAST** AT HIS POOR CHOICE OF AN ADJECTIVE THAT ONE TIME.

IT'S LIKE I WAS SAYING TO MY CHAUFFEUR THIS MORNING--OBAMA JUST DOESN'T **UNDERSTAND** REAL AMERICANS AS WELL AS WE **HIGHLY-PAID MEDIA PRO-FESSIONALS** DO!

MY HOUSEHOLD STAFF **CONCURS!**

BUT--AS CONSEQUENTIAL AS THIS ISSUE MAY BE, THERE **ARE** OTHER FACTORS TO CONSIDER WHEN CHOOSING THE NEXT LEADER OF THE FREE WORLD--LIKE WHO **LOVES AMERICA THE MOST**...

NOT ONLY DO I **WEAR** A FLAG PIN--I STICK IT DIRECTLY INTO MY **BARE FLESH!**

WOW! HE **REALLY** LOVES AMERICA!

MORE THAN OBAMA-- **THAT'S** FOR SURE!

TOM TOMORROW©2008

146

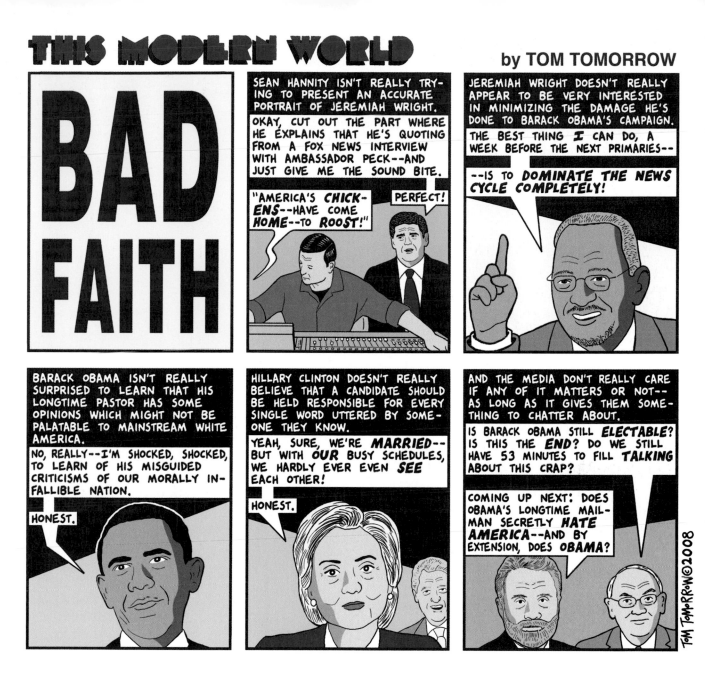

147

THIS MODERN WORLD

by TOM TOMORROW

SO IT TURNS OUT THAT THE ABUSE OF DETAINEES REALLY *CAN* BE BLAMED ON A HANDFUL OF "BAD APPLES"--AND THEIR NAMES ARE *CHENEY, RICE, RUMSFELD, POWELL, ASHCROFT* AND *TENET.*

WE NOW KNOW FOR A *FACT* THAT THEY ALL MET WITH CIA OFFICERS IN 2002 TO DISCUSS SPECIFIC INTERROGATION TECHNIQUES SUCH AS WATERBOARDING--AND THEN GAVE THE GREEN LIGHT FOR THOSE TECHNIQUES TO BE *USED.*

WHEN ASKED ABOUT THOSE MEETINGS, GEORGE BUSH SAID HE KNEW ABOUT THEM--AND HE *APPROVED.*

NOW, YOU MIGHT THINK AN OPEN ACKNOWLEDGMENT THAT TORTURE WAS, IN FACT, AN OFFICIAL POLICY OF THE UNITED STATES GOVERNMENT...WOULD BE KIND OF A BIG NEWS STORY.

BUT APPARENTLY, YOU WOULD BE MISTAKEN.

OUR TOP STORY TONIGHT--IS BARACK OBAMA AN ELITIST OR *WHAT?*

OUR EXPERTS DEBATE: IS "BITTERGATE" THE MOST IMPORTANT POLITICAL STORY OF THE *YEAR?*

AND--ARE AMERICANS *REALLY* READY FOR A PRESIDENT WHO *ISN'T A VERY GOOD BOWLER?*

FIRST THESE MESSAGES.

Action McNews Network

Tom Tomorrow ©2008

Outside the Castro Theatre, San Francisco, November 2007. (Passers-by were invited to text in their own messages to fill in Dick Cheney's word balloon.

ACKNOWLEDGMENTS: Special thanks to Carl Bromley, Robert Kimzey, and Sam Stoloff, all of whom were instrumental in making this latest volume a reality. Thanks also to Tony Ortega at the *Village Voice*, for kicking my ass until I made good on a drunken promise to deliver a cover piece on Bill O'Reilly; to Bob Harris, Jon Schwarz, and Greg Saunders for helping to feed the incessantly hungry blog; to Becky Bond at Credo, for making the photograph above possible; and to Violet Blue, for allowing me to reprint it. Finally, an inexpressible debt of gratitude is owed to one Beverly Gage for providing endless insight and inspiration, without which this book would be much thinner, and far less interesting.